TURKISH DELIGHT

by

JEREMY REED

HEARING EYE

HEARING EYE

Torriano Meeting House Poetry Pamphlet No.13
ISBN 1 870841 33 6
© Jeremy Reed (1993)

Jeremy Reed is well-known as a poet, novelist and non-fiction writer. He has published 25 books to date. His most recent collection of poetry is Red Haired Android, published by Harper Collins in 1992.

Titles published in this series:
A Bit of Dialect by A. C. Jacobs
Boogie Woogie by Jane Duran
Maurice V's Dido by E. A. Markham
Ventriloquism by Brian Docherty
St. Pancras Wells by Dinah Livingstone
Poems by Adam Johnson
Rock Pool by Anthony Edkins
Venetian Red by Sue Hubbard
Finding the Prince by Katherine Gallagher
Samizdat by David Kuhrt
Virtual Reality by Kathleen McPhilemy
Poems from Alonnisos by Simon Darragh

Hearing Eye, Box 1, 99 Torriano Avenue, London NW5 2RX

TURKISH DELIGHT

The sorbet tastes of rain on mulberry leaves,
summer as it's compacted into juice
sheathing the tongue: a purple cone.
the jet over from Dubai seems too near,

and if someone waved from low altitude
the conjectural gesture remains
of a hand opening above the landscape.
'Jeanette only wears pointed bras,' you say,
and now everything's clearer. I may think
the button pulls taut under strain
or the yoke's lifted fractionally. I hear
air waves from two conflicting radios
create a schizoid dialogue,
a metalanguage upending the seam
I think along. The sky's a clearer blue.

After the sorbet, it's turkish delight,
the little game we play, senses alert
to zones that tingle. We will end upstairs,
hearing a later jet, the engine tone
shifting on just another routine flight.

APPROACHING FRONTIERS

You left your red shoes with the border-guard,
or was that in a painting, I forget,
and in whose studio? Sometimes I go

wide of the understanding which I have,
and find your feet appealing when your toes
are meshed in a stocking's black point.
The country that we crossed to was a place
where big blue cats prowled tamely and we found
two people performing behind dry ice
in a tree-theatre off the road. They were
the last survivors of a race that wound
its grass-roots right across a continent
to a heart beating in a buried pot.

We never returned to the guard. The space
we took for the sky was orange,
an ad pulsing in a cloud, and we went
barefoot like children in the sand
counting our steps through crazy cactus land.

BILLIE HOLIDAY

Reworking cadence, when she finds the note
it's always different, singing without words
at the Apollo, letting her drift float

with the blue smoke plumes from a cigarette.
Style's in her spacing of words, Lady Day
a white flower in her hair, leading the set

wherever breath dictates, a mussed lipstick
tinting the song, one hand placing a glass
back on the piano top. It's not a trick

to catch the spotlight, but a need. Up there
her isolation is complete, she finds
a means to centre it, and takes us where

there's consolation for a spike-heeled fall
into back alley junk. "Gloomy Sunday"
is slowed to speech. Leaning against the wall

her back contains the storm. She feels the past
as a pivotal hurricane, and lets
the saxophonist punctuate the cast

of figures she inhabits; it is hard,
maintaining poise, creating out of pain,
bowing out at the end as a reward.

NEO DADAIST COCKTAIL

The basement's ratted. Where the skinheads lit
a fire, they've blackened in a swastika,
a prescient deathshead sits on the wall,
the more dramatic for its orange eyes,
beer cans are punched into this dialect,
declared credo, Search and Destroy.
The gang hung out there, drew chains to elect
a grizzled leader, saw the metaphor
extend beyond Hitler's bunker
to their underground hideaway, a lair
from which to issue on nocturnal raids,
unzip the precinct's loaded seam.
A post punk blitzkrieg. They adopted names,
Blank Harry, Slash and Burn, Razorblade Jim,
and territorialized the neighbourhood,
their marks were looted windows, a sharp point
tattooed over a car's metallic sheen,
graffiti sprayed up to outlaw the rich,
a wild recriminative vocabulary,
spit in the teeth vehemence. When they left,
their ghetto blaster wrecked, one signed himself
Psycho Fuhrer, They cut into the night,
a pack hunting through side streets, born to lose,
but in the process putting up a fight.

SPACE CAKE

A ladder telescopes into the sky,
a pear-shaped ruby balanced on the top.
I notate Michaux's drawings. Jane gets thin
by thinking herself vertically
into the scarlet anemone's stem,
the one that visibly draws on water
to combat entropy. All the way up.

The window opposite's a cat's square eye,
a rectangular buttercup.
It stays there half the night. I've seen the man
collect and recollect a glass
attempting to kill consciousness, too high
to enter sleep by a white door
and float bareback above a violet fish
so fluent it is water.
                    I look out

on every possibility
that interacts with my space chemistry.
Two blue sheets on the washing line
are small sharks mating. I've been up two days
travelling inwardly. The desert's wings
lift to reveal the sea. The last signpost
directs me to the refrigerator,
the cool juice blazing on decantation -
an orange lighthouse sitting in a glass
I hold to a night in which ships are lost.

STONE LADDER

A bouldered zigzag trail into the hills;
his jeep high-stepped the worst, the lizards lay
like twitching spines along each stone,
demented lightning prickles when disturbed.

At night his headlights pushed furred moons
into the dark. Sometimes one, often two
silent watchers awaited him
drinking whiskey in white cane rocking chairs,

the woman hardly dressed, the boy
with marmoset's eyes, carving a canoe
from bark, arrogating control
over the edgy scene, letting a shoe

drop in the silence like a dice
prognosticating who would speak. The let
was in her smile, the smudged lipstick,
the clicking ricochet she gave to ice

that tinkled in the glass. He'd read her mood
instinctively, the bruised pansy
his or the boy's lips had coloured,
was livid indigo along her neck.

They'd hear him unloading outside,
and sit there tense, acquisitive. Tonight
he stayed out a long time. Stones from the peak
were moving again in a lithic tide.

WRITING TO

A blue day opens out into a red.
An afternoon spent up on the third floor
meant reading Strindberg's mania,
the lyricism all pathologized,
the stars and stripes duvet, the black curtains
unfurling like flags with a breeze
from nowhere. Just the empty sky

waiting the way a blank cinema screen
seems ordinary without images.
And after the scenario, credits,
we see a woman tying up her hair,
a man sits watching her, he's still in bed,
despite the Paris or the Berlin day.
His green jacket's hung over a white chair.
Her black bra is transparent lace.
She smiles, and now the music starts to play.

It's been like that for hours. Cinematic,
post-coital. My green-eyed look
goes once around the universe
and back to you. I hear you turn a page.
You're reading by wishing you had a book.

GREEN MOODS

A different temper to blue, a shade
denoting a slight up on solitude,
a green movie, a green hour, a green mood,
it's a new flavour for the cocktail straw
through which we savour life. The clear postmark
tells me your letter was a year coming,
and so much happened in between, I saw

a plateau overtaken by the sea,
and when it withdrew there were triton shells,
tufted manes of emerald weed,
a mise-en-scène, an improvised
marine canvas by Yves Tanguy.

I juggle a blue ball and then a green.
Your eyeliner takes up with the latter;
mascara always smells of writing ink.
The bottle-green sky moves in by mid-afternoon.
Those who anticipate it go on out
walking to nowhere, or else take a train
to a city whose name I cannot spell,
except its walls are green, its occupants

square headed. It's an individual thing,
the texture deepens after summer rain.